NORTH AMERICAN MAMMALS

# Prairie Dog

Jinny Johnson

# Contents

Published by Smart Apple Media,
an imprint of Black Rabbit Books
P.O. Box 3263, Mankato, Minnesota, 56002
www.blackrabbitbooks.com

U.S. publication copyright © 2014 Smart Apple Media.
International copyright reserved in all countries.
No part of this book may be reproduced in any form
without written permission from the publisher.

Printed in the United States of America,
at Corporate Graphics in North Mankato, Minnesota.

Designed by Hel James
Edited by Mary-Jane Wilkins

Cataloging-in-Publication Data
is available from the Library of Congress

ISBN 978-1-62588-034-5

Photo acknowledgements
t = top, b = bottom
title page Peter Gudella/Shutterstock; page 3 l i g h t p o e t /
Shutterstock; 5 iStockphoto/Thinkstock; 6 iStockphoto/
Thinkstock; 7 Hemera/Thinkstock; 8 iStockphoto/Thinkstock;
10 Darrell J. Rohl/Shutterstock; 11, 12 iStockphoto/Thinkstock;
14 Ognian/Shutterstock; 15, 16 iStockphoto/Thinkstock;
17 John Cancalosi/ardea.com; 18 Ryan Ladbrook/Shutterstock;
19 Colette3/Shutterstock; 20, 21 Henk Bentlage/Shutterstock;
22t James Marvin Phelps, b Eric Isselee/both Shutterstock;
23 Henk Bentlage/Shutterstock
Cover Bettina Baumgartner/Shutterstock

DAD0509
052013
9 8 7 6 5 4 3 2 1

I'm a black-tailed prairie dog.

I live on the grasslands of North America.

# My Family

Did you know that I'm not a dog at all? I'm a kind of squirrel that lives on the ground. Prairie dogs do make a sound that's like a dog's bark though.

I live with my family in an underground burrow. There's my mom and dad, my aunties, and my brothers and sisters.

**Our Home**

Our burrow is not just a tunnel. It has several entrances and different "rooms." There are places for sleeping and we line these with dried grass and leaves.

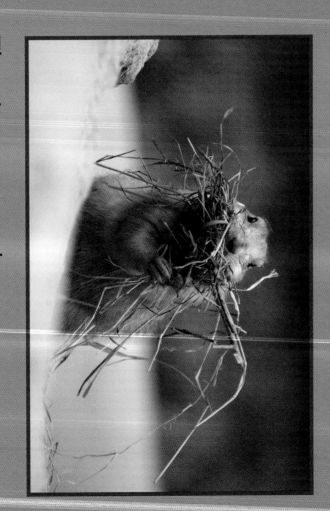

There's a nursery where my mom looked after us when we were little and there are places where we store food. We even have a toilet area, where we pee and poop.

# First Weeks

My sisters and I were born in our burrow, in the nursery area. We were tiny and helpless.

**Mom fed us with her milk for about six weeks and kept us clean.**

Our dad didn't help to look after us but he did watch out for the whole family. My mom was fierce and didn't let other prairie dogs into the nursery.

# Our Day

Now we are old enough to come out and find our own food. We pop up above ground in the morning.

We spend the day feeding, playing, and grooming ourselves and each other. Mom and dad check the burrow entrances and make repairs.

In summer we go back underground to sleep during the hottest part of the day. In cooler weather we may stay out until the evening.

# Favorite Food

We eat leaves, roots, and stems of grasses and other plants.

We sometimes gobble up some insects, such as grasshoppers, as we feed.

We don't really need to drink water. We get all the liquid we need from our food.

# Look Out!

Lots of other prairie dog families live nearby in their own burrows.

Our whole group is called a colony. While we are all out feeding, one member of our colony keeps an eye out for danger.

If a predator comes too close, the lookout gives an alarm call and we all dive back into our burrows. We stay out of sight until someone checks and makes the all-clear call.

# Keeping in Touch

We "talk" to each other with lots of sounds and calls.

We even make different calls to warn about different predators.

When the lookout calls an alarm, it tells the rest of us whether the threat is from a coyote, a ferret, or other animals. We even know whether the predator is big or small.

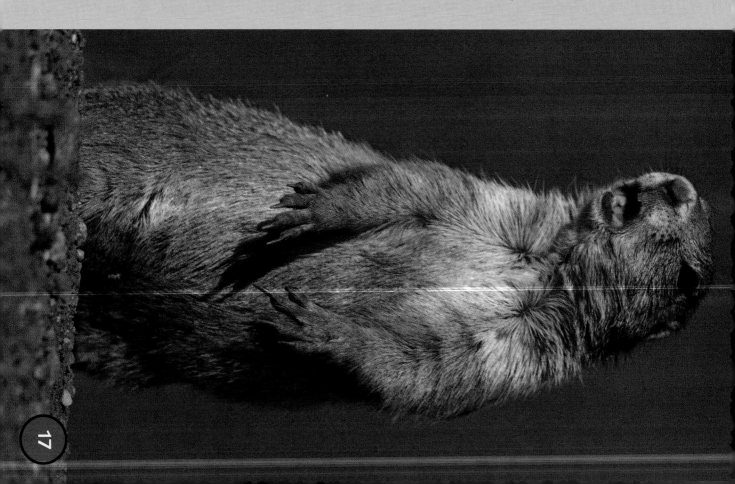

# Furry and Friendly

I have a chubby body, brown fur, and a tail with a black tip.

My legs are short and I have strong sharp claws to help me dig burrows.

My eyes are very big and black.

We prairie dogs are generally very friendly to each other, except when we have young to protect. When we meet we touch noses. It looks like we are kissing.

# Leaving Home

My sister will stay with family. Males like me leave and join another family when we are about two years old.

I will have young of my own and protect them from danger, just like my dad did for me.

# Prairie Dog Facts

Prairie dogs are rodents, like rats and mice, and they belong to the squirrel family. There are five species and they all live in North America.

An average prairie dog is about 12 inches (30 cm) long, with a tail of about 4 inches (10 cm). It weighs about 2 pounds (1 kg).

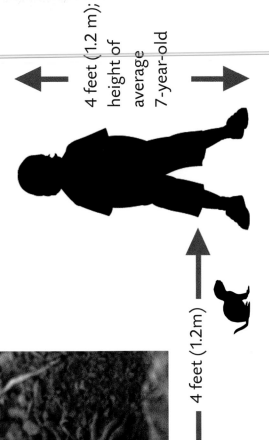

4 feet (1.2 m); height of average 7-year-old

4 feet (1.2m)

Utah prairie dog

Once millions of black-tailed prairie dogs lived in colonies that spread over many miles. Now colonies are much smaller, with fewer animals.

## Useful Words

**colony** A group of animals of the same kind that live close together.

**groom** To care for and clean the fur.

**predator** An animal that lives by catching and eating other animals.

## Index

## Web Link

Learn more about prairie dogs at
www.sandiegozoo.org/animalbytes/t-prairie_dog